I0887166

Breathe Easy II

LEISURE ARTS, INC. • Maumelle, Arkansas

Introduction

So, if we're going to wear masks why not make them stylish and fashionable? This book features quick, cute masks that will keep your people protected while also being a one-of-a-kind fashion accessory. We give you a variety of mask types and embellishment techniques to choose from to make your mask unique and original. Just pick a mask type from pages 36–43 and then choose an embellishment technique to complete your mask. And as a bonus we give you 3 cute options for keeping your ears comfy. These masks won't just be useful, they'll keep you in style, too!

Contents

SUNFLOWER
OLFA PATENTED

Social
Influencer

All dressed up

Vinyl

Electric cutting machines make it super simple to cut heat transfer vinyl designs for masks. And with a myriad of colors and patterns, there's no limit to what you can do.

1. Follow **Shaped Mask Assembly**, page 38, or **Pleated Mask Assembly**, page 42, to complete mask.

2. Follow your cutting machine's instructions and use heat transfer vinyl to cut designs for your masks. Go to the links below and size as desired.

   bit.ly/L7741_Buck
   bit.ly/L7741_Truck
   bit.ly/L7741_Social-Influencer
   bit.ly/L7741_Sun
   bit.ly/L7741_All-Dressed-Up
   bit.ly/L7741_Unicorn
   bit.ly/L7741_Deer-Mount

3. Follow the vinyl manufacturer's instructions to apply the vinyl design to your mask.

BONUS: TIED EAR PROTECTOR

1. For ear protector, cut 2 strips 2½" x 26". Refer to **Fig. 1** to trim ends of each strip to a tapered point.

2. Using a ¼" seam allowance, sew strips together, leaving an opening for turning. Turn right side out and press; sew opening closed.

3. Tie ear protector around head. Mark placement for buttons on each side. Sew buttons to ear protector.

Fig. 1

Machine Appliqué

Preparing Fusible Appliqués

White or light-colored fabrics may need to be lined with fusible interfacing before applying fusible web to prevent darker fabrics from showing through.

1. Our appliqué patterns are printed in reverse. Place paper-backed fusible web, paper side up, over appliqué pattern. Trace pattern onto paper side of web with pencil.
2. Follow manufacturer's instructions to fuse traced patterns to wrong side of fabrics. Do not remove paper backing.
3. Use scissors to cut out appliqué pieces along traced lines.

Adding the Appliqués

1. Follow **Shaped Mask Assembly**, page 38, Steps 1–2 and 3 (optional) or **Pleated Mask Assembly**, page 42, Step 1 (optional), to make mask body and lining.
2. Arrange the appliqués on the mask body. Be sure to keep the appliqué out of the seam allowances and at least 1" from the side edges. Fuse the appliqués in place.
3. Pin stabilizer, such as paper or any of the commercially available products, on wrong side of mask body fabric before stitching appliqués in place.
4. Thread sewing machine with general-purpose thread; use general-purpose thread that matches body fabric in bobbin.
5. Stitch around appliqués using a straight stitch, blanket stitch, or any decorative machine stitch desired. Do not backstitch at end of stitching. Pull threads to wrong side of body fabric; knot thread and trim ends.
6. Carefully tear away stabilizer.
7. Follow **Shaped Mask Assembly**, page 38, Steps 4–6, or **Pleated Mask Assembly**, page 42, Steps 2–4, to complete mask.

Machine Appliqué Patterns

Patterns are also available as SVG files to be used with an electronic cutting machine that cuts fabric. Adhere paper-backed fusible web to wrong side of fabric before cutting. Here are the SVG links:

bit.ly/L7741_Turtle
bit.ly/L7741_Bird
bit.ly/L7741_Flower
bit.ly/L7741_Leaves
bit.ly/L7741_Butterfly

Turtles

Bird

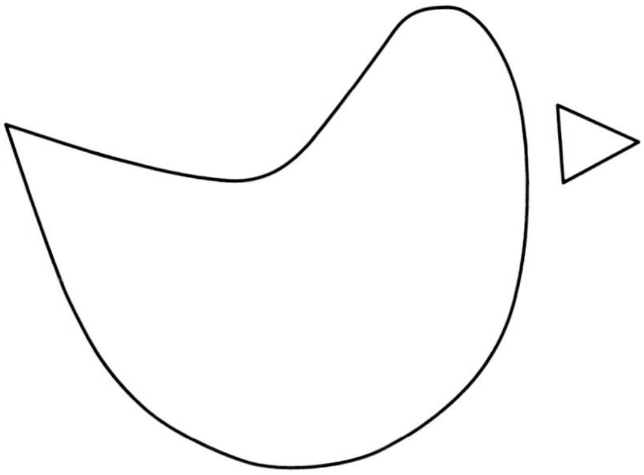

Flowers

Machine Appliqué Patterns, *continued*

Leaves

Butterfly

60°

BIAS
60

Diamond Dotz®

Use Diamond Dotz® Premium Resin Dotz® to add some sparkle to any fabric. We chose areas of the fabric to embellish based on the design of the fabric—over dots in the fabric, defining the parts of a flower, or scattered individually on the fabric. With thousands of colors to choose from, you'll be able to add gems that coordinate with any fabric to give your mask some pizzazz.

1. Follow **Shaped Mask Assembly**, page 38, or **Pleated Mask Assembly**, page 42, to complete mask.

2. Use Diamond Dotz® All Purpose Dotting Adhesive, a Diamond Dotz® Wax Pot, and a Diamond Dotz® Stylus to adhere Diamond Dotz® to the fabric.

   If placing Diamond Dotz in a large area, for example, filling the area of a flower, use a small paintbrush to carefully brush the adhesive on the area where you wish to apply gems. You should see a milky white layer of adhesive on the surface. Allow the adhesive to dry until it is clear. When adhesive clears completely it is ready for long term adhesion. Use the stylus to apply the gems to the adhesive as desired.

   If placing individual gems randomly, use a small round paintbrush to place dots of adhesive where you wish to apply gems. You should see a milky white layer of adhesive on the surface. Allow the adhesive to dry until it is clear. When adhesive clears completely it is ready for long term adhesion. Use the stylus to apply the gems to the adhesive.

3. After you have added the gems, firmly roll over the whole design with a brayer or rolling pin. This ensures that the gems are firmly adhered.

BONUS:
HEADBAND EAR PROTECTOR

1. Using headband pattern below, cut headband front and lining from fabric. For casing, cut 2 fabric strips 1¾" x 10". From 1" wide elastic, cut a 6" long piece.
2. For headband, sew front and lining together along long curved edges. Turn right side out and press. Press short ends of headband ¼" to inside.
3. For casing, match right sides and sew strips together along long edges. Turn right side out and press.
4. Using a safety pin, insert elastic in casing, aligning ends of elastic with ends of casing. Baste across ends of casing to hold elastic.
5. Place ends of casing in ends of headband; pin. Topstitch along edges of headband, catching ends of casing as you sew.
6. Sew a button at each end of headband front for attaching elastic ear loops.

Pattern

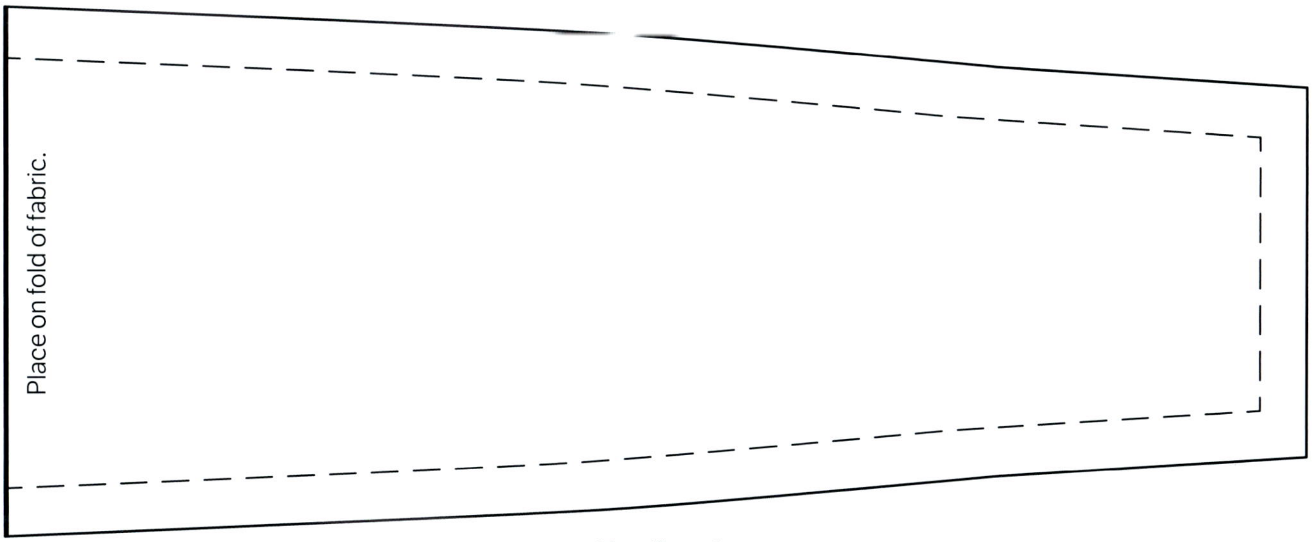

Headband

busy

SUNFLOWER

Stitchery

Embellish your mask with sweet embroidery or cross stitch.

Embroidery

1. Follow **Shaped Mask Assembly**, page 38, Step 1, to cut mask pieces.
2. Place mask body pieces over pattern as desired and trace pattern to mask body piece using a water-soluble fabric marker.
3. Refer to **Stitch Diagrams** to embroider desired design following the **Color/Stitch Guide**.
4. Follow **Shaped Mask Assembly**, page 38, Steps 2–6, to complete mask.

Stitch Diagrams

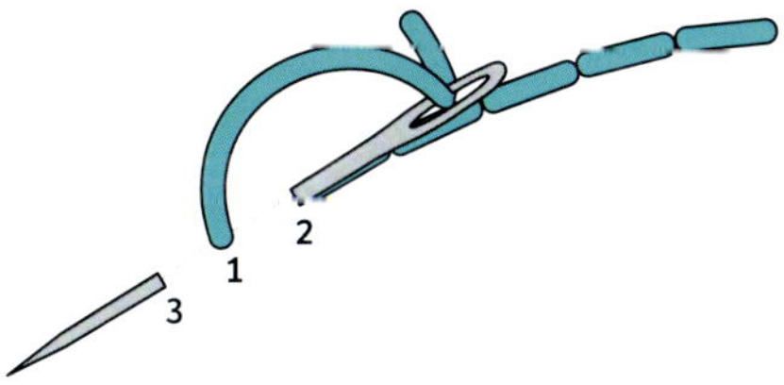

Backstitch

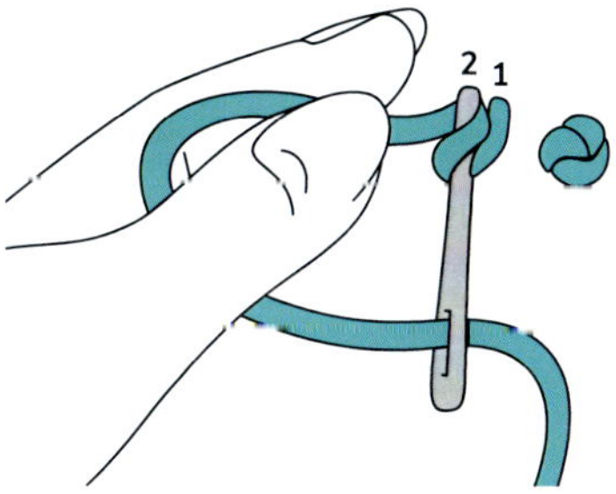

French Knot

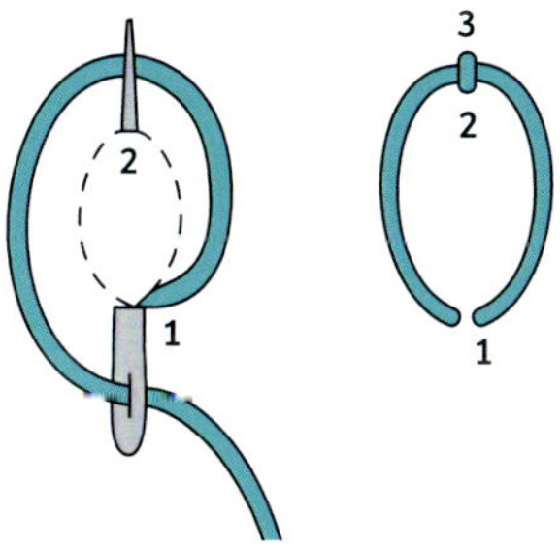

Lazy Daisy Stitch

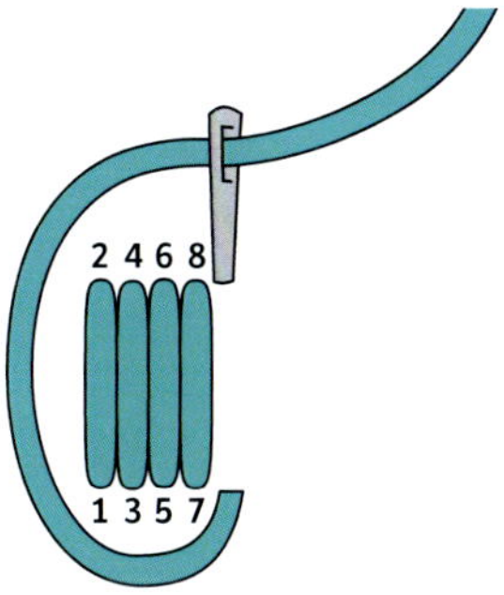

Satin Stitch

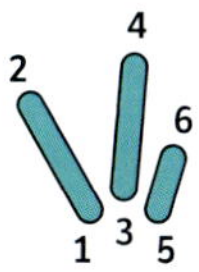

Straight Stitch

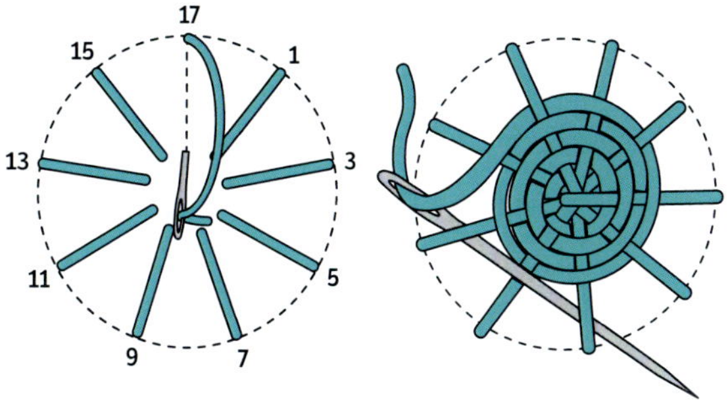

Woven Wheel

BUSY BEE

Color/Stitch Guide

- Use 3 strands of floss to work Backstitches for word, antennae, wings, and body.
- Use 1 strand of floss to work Backstitches for head, mouth, and around eyes.
- Use 3 strands for all French Knots and Satin Stitches.
- Add a decorative wooden flower button to the mask body.

Pattern

Gold

BEE SAFE

Color/Stitch Guide

- Use 3 strands of floss to work all stitches.
- Work Satin Stitches for bee body and wings.
- Work Backstitches for words, stems, and bee outline.
- Work Running Stitches for bee trail.
- Work Straight Stitches for antennae and small flower leaves.
- Work Lazy Daisy Stitches for each leaf and flower petal; work smaller Lazy Daisy Stitches inside each leaf and flower petal to fill the space.
- Work French Knots for large purple flowers and small flower centers.

Pattern

BEE CALM

Color/Stitch Guide

- Use 3 strands of floss to work all stitches.
- Work Satin Stitches for bee body and wings.
- Work Backstitches for words, stems, and bee outline.
- Work Running Stitches for bee trail.
- Work Straight Stitches for antennae, small flower leaves, and flower pistils.
- Work Lazy Daisy Stitches for each leaf and flower petal; work smaller Lazy Daisy Stitches inside each leaf and flower petal to fill the space.
- Work Woven Wheel Roses for large flowers.
- Work French Knots in large flower centers and small flower pistils.

White | Pink | Yellow | Green | Dark Red | Black

Pattern

BEE WELL

Color/Stitch Guide

- Use 3 strands of floss to work all stitches.
- Work Satin Stitches for each daisy center, bee body, and bee wings.
- Work Backstitches for words, stems, bee outline, and daisy center outline.
- Work Running Stitches for bee trail.
- Work Straight Stitches for antennae, small flower leaves, and flower pistils.
- Work Lazy Daisy Stitches for each leaf and flower petal; work smaller Lazy Daisy Stitches inside each leaf and flower petal to fill the space.
- Work French Knots for small flower pistils.

Pattern

BEE STRONG

Color/Stitch Guide

- Use 3 strands of floss to work all stitches.
- Work Satin Stitches for bee body and wings.
- Work Backstitches for words, stems, and bee outline.
- Work Running Stitches for bee trail.
- Work Straight Stitches for antennae and small flower leaves.
- Work Lazy Daisy Stitches for each leaf and flower petal; work smaller Lazy Daisy Stitches inside each leaf and flower petal to fill the space.
- Work brown French Knots in sunflower centers and yellow French Knots in small flowers.

White Yellow Orange Green Black

Pattern

Cross Stitch

HOW TO READ CHARTS

The chart is made up of a key and a charted design on which each square represents a stitch. The symbols in the key tell which floss color to use for each stitch in the chart. The following headings and symbols are given:

X—Cross Stitch

B'ST—Backstitch

DMC—DMC color number

COLOR—The name given to the floss color in the chart

A square filled with a color and a symbol should be worked as a **Cross Stitch**.

A straight line should be worked as a **Backstitch**.

GETTING STARTED

Waste Canvas

Waste canvas is a special canvas that provides an evenweave grid for placing stitches on fabric. After the design is worked over the canvas, the canvas threads are removed, leaving the design on the fabric.

Preparing Fabric

Cut a 5" x 5" piece of 10 mesh waste canvas. Cover edges of waste canvas with masking tape. Cut a 6" x 6" piece of chambray fabric and lightweight, non-fusible interfacing.

Find desired stitching area on chambray and mark center of area with a pin. Match center of canvas to pin on chambray. With canvas threads straight, pin canvas to right side of chambray; pin interfacing to wrong side. Baste all three thicknesses together.

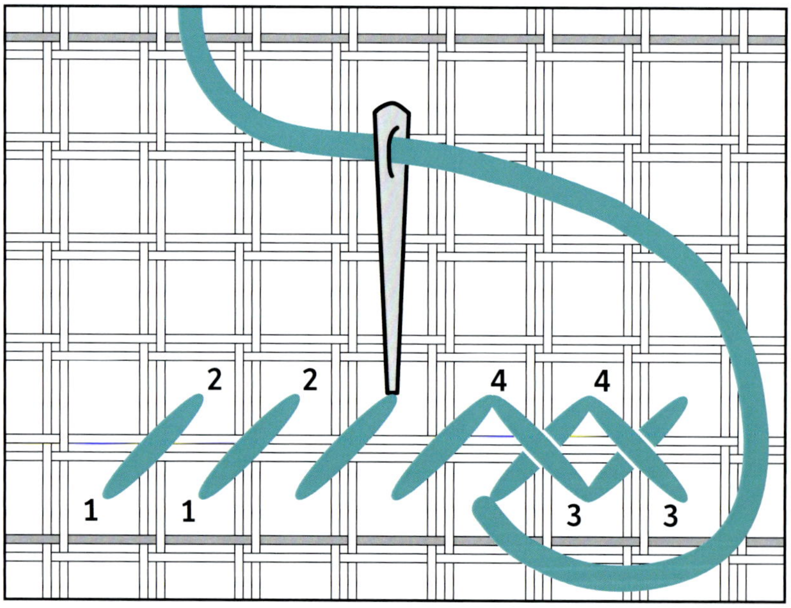

Fig. 1

Working with Floss

To ensure smoother stitches, separate strands; then realign them before threading the needle. Keep stitching tension consistent. Begin and end floss by running under several stitches on the back; never tie knots.

Where to Start

The horizontal and vertical center of the charted design is shown by arrows pointing to the center. You may start at any point on the charted design, but be sure the design will be centered on the fabric. Locate the center of the fabric by folding it in half, top to bottom and again left to right. On the charted design, count the number of squares (stitches) from the center of the chart to where you wish to start. Then, from the fabric's center, find your starting point by counting out the same number of fabric threads (stitches).

How to Stitch

Always work Cross Stitches first; then add the Backstitch. When stitching, bring the threaded needle up at 1 and all odd numbers and down at 2 and all even numbers.

Cross Stitch: For horizontal rows, work stitches in two journeys (**Fig. 1**). For vertical rows, complete each stitch as shown (**Fig. 2**).

Backstitch: For outlines and details, Backstitch should be worked after the design has been completed (**Fig. 3**).

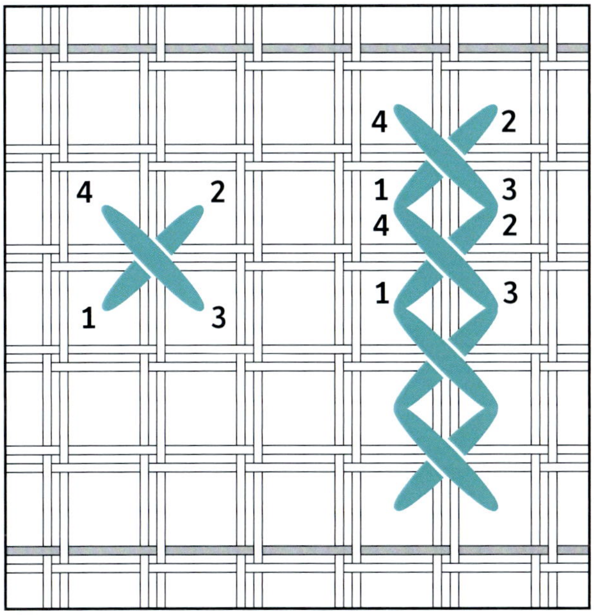

Fig. 2

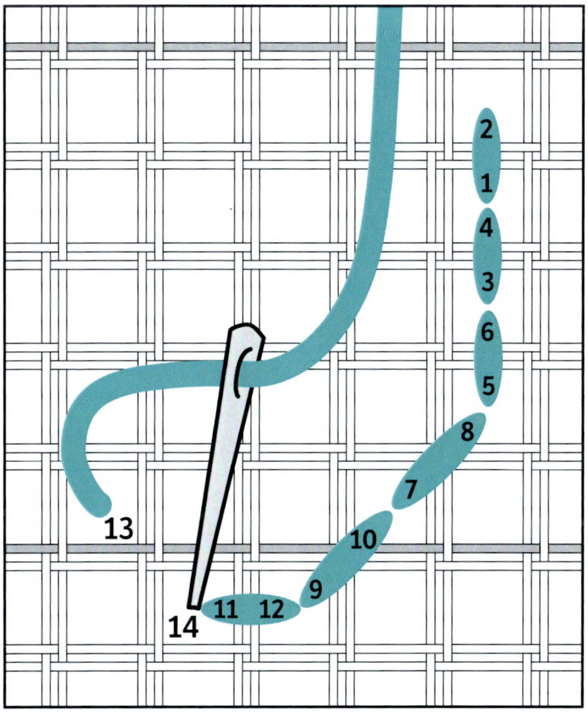

Fig. 3

SUNFLOWER
OLFA PATENTED

SUNFLOWER MASK

1. Follow **Shaped Mask Assembly**, page 38, to make mask.

2. Place basted waste canvas, chambray, and interfacing in hoop. Using a sharp needle, work design, stitching from large holes to large holes.

3. Trim canvas to within ¾" of design. Dampen canvas until it becomes limp. Pull out canvas threads one at a time using tweezers. Trim interfacing close to design.

4. Trim chambray ⅛" outside stitched design. Zigzag stitch the chambray to the mask.

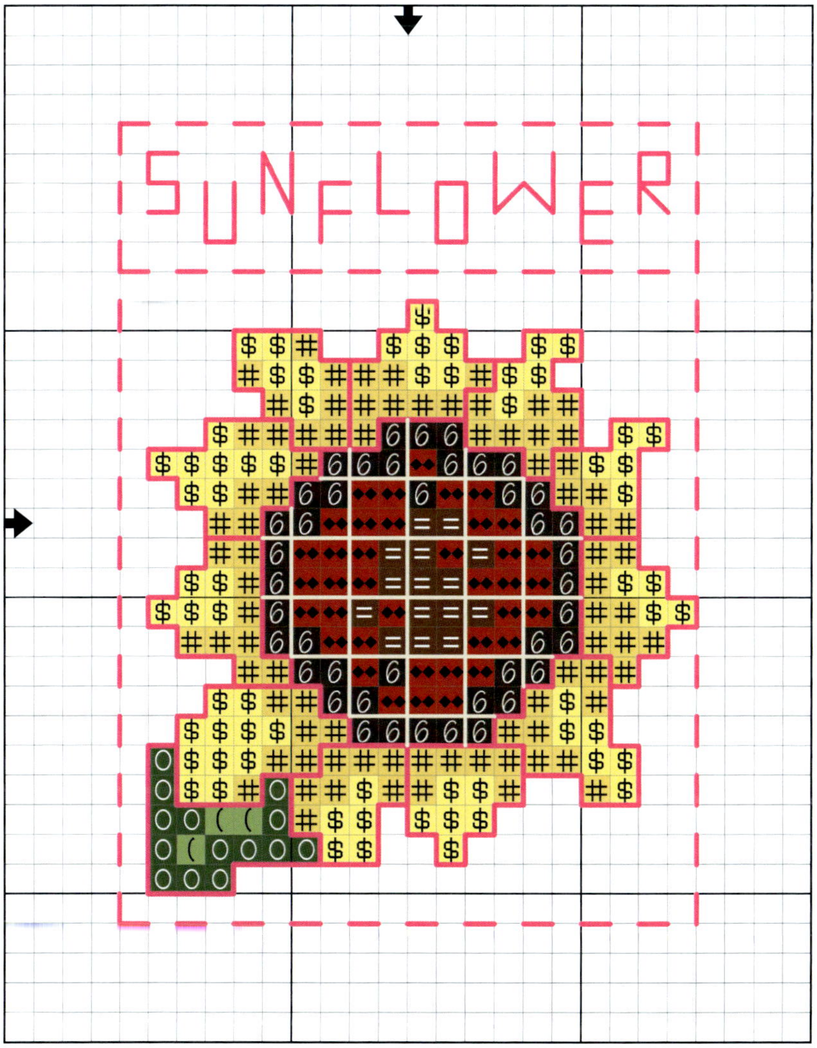

Design by Susan Fouts

Sunflower Key

Stitch Count: 20w x 27h
Design Size: 2" x 2¾"

CROSS STITCH—2 strands

X	DMC	Color
••	433	Brown
=	434	Light Brown
(	471	Light Green
#	725	Dark Yellow
$	726	Yellow
6	801	Dark Brown
O	3346	Green

BACKSTITCH—1 strand

B'st	DMC	Color
/	310	Black
/	Ecru	Ecru

Simple Sewing

Adding Ribbon or Trim

1. Follow **Shaped Mask**, page 36 or **Pleated Mask**, page 40, to cut mask pieces.

2. Sew ribbon or trim along the top and/or bottom of the mask body **(photos A and B)**, across the mask body **(photo C)**, or anywhere desired on the mask body **(photo D)**. Ribbon or trim can be stitched into the folds of a pleated mask body. If desired, ribbon or trim can be stitched along the edges of the finished mask **(photo E)**.

A

B

C

D

E

Patchwork

1. From solid black fabric, cut 2 large rectangles 3" x 6¾" and 2 small rectangles 1¼" x 6¾". Cut 10 solid yellow squares and 10 assorted print squares 2¼" x 2¼".

2. Draw a diagonal line on wrong side of each solid square. With right sides together, place 1 solid square on top of 1 print square. Stitch ¼" from each side of drawn line (**Fig. 1**).

3. Cut along drawn line and press seam allowances toward the print fabric to make 2 Triangle Squares. Make 20 **Triangle Squares**. Trim each Triangle-Square to 1¾" x 1¾".

4. Sew 5 triangle squares together to make a **Row**. Make 4 Rows. Sew 2 Rows together to make **Unit 1**. Make 2 Unit 1's.

5. Sew 1 small rectangle and 1 large rectangle to Unit 1 to make **Unit 2**. Make 2 Unit 2's.

6. Follow **Shaped Mask Assembly**, page 38, to complete mask. When cutting mask body from Unit 2, place pattern so that patchwork area is placed on mask as desired.

Fig. 1

Triangle Square (make 20)

Row (make 4)

Unit 1 (make 2)

Unit 2 (make 2)

BONUS: RIBBON EAR SAVER

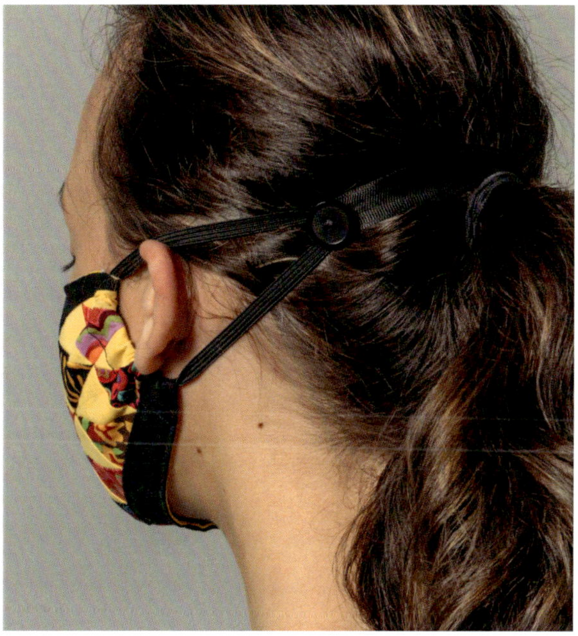

1. From grosgrain ribbon, cut a 12" piece.
2. Fold 1 end of ribbon under ½". Overlap folded end over raw end about ½"; machine stitch ends together to form a circle.
3. With overlapped ends of ribbon centered on 1 side, flatten loop. Sew a button to each end of ribbon loop for attaching elastic ear loops.

Shaped Mask

Shopping List

- ☐ Prewashed and dried 100% cotton fabric for mask body and lining
  - Large Adult—two 8" x 7" pieces
  - Small Adult—two 7" x 7" pieces
  - Child—two 6" x 6" pieces
- ☐ Prewashed and dried lightweight or featherweight non-woven interfacing (not fusible)
  - Large Adult—two 8" x 7" pieces
  - Small Adult—two 7" x 7" pieces
  - Child—two 6"x 6" pieces
- ☐ Sewing machine
- ☐ Matching/coordinating sewing thread
- ☐ Tracing paper and pen or pencil

OPTIONS

- ☐ Prewashed and dried 100% cotton fabric for interior filter pocket—8" x 7" piece of fabric
- ☐ Two 40" lengths of ribbon, twill tape, or 2" wide strips of t-shirt fabric for ties (Style 1)
- ☐ 1¼ yds of paracord and a cord lock clamp for ties (Style 2)
- ☐ ⅛" or ¼" wide elastic (Style 3 or 4)—16" length (Style 3) or 25" length (Style 4)
- ☐ Small paper clip to allow mask to be shaped around nose

Style 1—*This mask has ties on the sides that tie around the head.* Complete Steps 1, 2, 3 (optional), and 4.

Style 2—*This mask has paracord on the sides and a cord lock clamp to secure the mask around the head.* Complete Steps 1, 2, 3 (optional), and 4.

Style 3—*This mask has elastic ear loops.* Complete Steps 1, 2, 3 (optional), and 5.

Style 4—*This mask has a continuous elastic loop.* Complete Steps 1, 2, 3 (optional), and 6.

1

1

2

2

2

3

4

Shaped Mask Assembly

Always use a ¼" seam allowance unless otherwise indicated.

1. Trace the desired size pattern (pages 46–48); cut out traced pattern. Use the pattern to cut the 2 mask body pieces from fabric, 2 lining pieces from fabric, and 4 interfacing pieces. ***If a pocket is desired,*** cut 2 pocket pieces from fabric. You can also cut the pieces with an electronic cutting machine; see page 46 for links.

2. Pin an interfacing piece to the wrong side of each mask body and lining piece. Matching right sides and raw edges, sew the center front seam of the mask body. Clip the curved seam allowances. Press the seam allowances to one side. Repeat to sew the center front seam of the lining, pressing the seam allowances so that they will be on the opposite side from the body. *Optional:* topstitch the seam allowances in place on each piece.

3. ***If you are adding a pocket to the lining of the mask,*** sew the center front seam of the pocket. Clip the curved seam and press the seam allowances open. Press the top edge of the pocket ½" to the wrong side, clipping as necessary. Topstitch in place. Matching wrong side of pocket to right side of lining, baste the pocket to the lining along the bottom and treat as one unit from now on (**photo A**).

4. ***If you would like to have ribbon, twill tape, t-shirt fabric, or paracord ties,*** match the center seams, place mask body and lining right sides together and sew the top and bottom edges. ***Optional:*** add a paper clip for nose shaping after sewing the top and bottom seams; see page 45. Clip the curved seam allowances. Turn the mask right side out and press. For the casing, press one short side ¼" toward the lining; press ½" toward the lining.

A

B

Topstitch close to the fold. Use a safety pin to thread the ribbon, twill tape, t-shirt strips (**photos B** and **C**) or paracord (**photo D**) ties through the casing. Knot ends of ties if desired. For paracord, add a cord lock clamp.

5. ***If you would like to have elastic ear loops,*** match the center seams and place mask body and lining right sides together; sew the top and bottom edges. *Optional:* add a paper clip for nose shaping after sewing the top and bottom seams; see page 45. Clip the curved seam allowances. Turn the mask right side out and press. For the elastic casing, press one short side ¼" toward the lining; press ½" toward the lining. Topstitch close to the fold. Use a safety pin to thread a 6"–8" length of elastic through the casing (**photo E**). Knot or sew the elastic ends together. Reposition the elastic so that the knot or sewn area is inside the casing. Repeat on the remaining short side.

6. ***If you would like to have a continuous elastic loop,*** match the center seams and place mask body and lining right sides together; sew the top and bottom edges. *Optional:* add a paper clip for nose shaping after sewing the top and bottom seams; see page 45. Clip the curved seam allowances. Turn the mask right side out and press. For the elastic casing, press one short side ¼" toward the lining; press ½" toward the lining. Topstitch close to the fold. Repeat on the remaining short side. Use a safety pin to thread a 16" length of elastic through the casings (**photo F**). Knot or sew the elastic ends together. Reposition the elastic so that the knot or sewn area is inside the casing.

C

D

E

F

Pleated Mask

Shopping List

- ☐ Prewashed and dried 100% cotton fabric for mask body and lining
  - Adult—two 9" x 6" pieces
  - Child—two 7½" x 5" pieces
- ☐ Prewashed and dried lightweight or featherweight non-woven interfacing (not fusible)
  - Adult—two 9" x 6" pieces
  - Child—two 7½" x 5" pieces
- ☐ Sewing machine
- ☐ Matching/coordinating sewing thread

OPTIONS

- ☐ Prewashed and dried 100% cotton fabric for interior filter pocket—9" x 6" piece of fabric
- ☐ Prewashed and dried 100% cotton fabric for ties (Style 1)—two 2" x 40" strips of fabric (can be cut from width of fabric or joined)
- ☐ Two 40" lengths of twill tape or ribbon for ties (Style 2 or 3)
- ☐ Small paper clip to allow mask to be shaped around nose

Style 1—*This mask has binding ties on the top and bottom of the mask that tie around the head.* Complete Steps 1 (optional) and 2.

Style 2—*This mask has twill tape ties on the sides of the mask that tie around the head.* Complete Steps 1 (optional) and 3.

Style 3—*This mask has ribbon ties on the sides of the mask that tie around the head.* Complete Steps 1 (optional) and 4.

1

2

3

Pleated Mask Assembly

Always use a ¼" seam allowance.

1. ***If you are adding a pocket to the back of the mask,*** press the top edge of the pocket ½" to the wrong side. Topstitch in place. Matching wrong side of pocket to right side of lining, baste the pocket to the lining along the bottom and treat as one unit from now on (**photo A**).

2. **If you would like to have binding ties on the top and bottom of the mask,** refer to **Making Binding for Ties**, page 44, to make binding ties for the mask. Pin an interfacing piece to the wrong side of mask body and lining piece. Place mask body and lining right sides together and sew the short ends. Turn the mask right side out and press.

   Optional: add a paper clip for nose shaping before adding the binding; see page 45. Press 3 pleats into the mask, folding and pressing all layers (**photo B**). Topstitch the pleats in place along the short ends. Matching the center of a binding strip to the center of the mask, pin the binding to the mask top, sandwiching the mask between the binding layers. Starting at one end of the binding, topstitch close to the open edges, continuing across the mask and to the opposite end of the binding (**photo C**). Repeat for the mask bottom.

3. ***If you would like to have twill tape ties on the sides of the mask,*** pin an interfacing piece to the wrong side of mask body and lining piece. Place

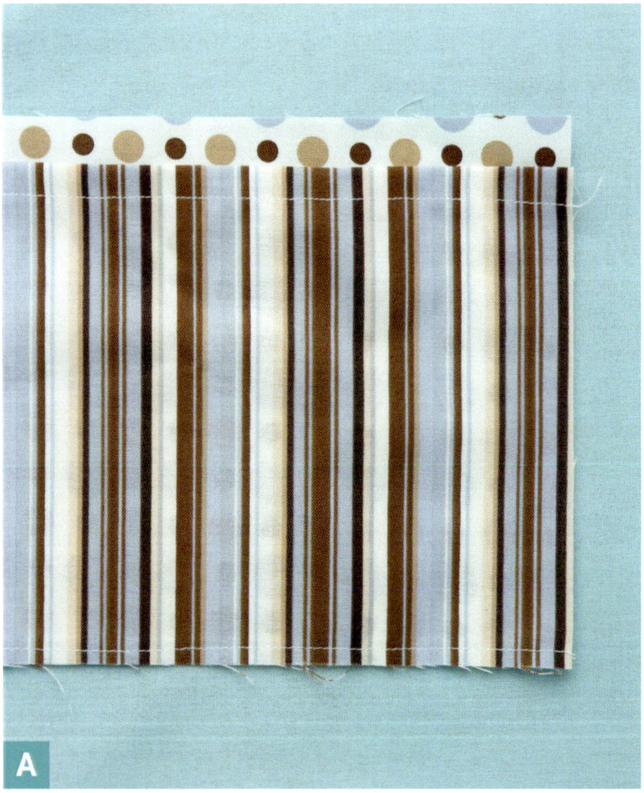

A

B

mask body and lining right sides together and sew the long edges. *Optional:* add a paper clip for nose shaping before adding the binding; see page 45. Turn the mask right side out and press. Press 3 pleats into the mask, folding and pressing all layers (**photo B**). Baste the pleats in place along the short ends. Matching the center of a twill tape to the center of one short end, fold the twill tape over the edge and pin to the mask, sandwiching the mask between the folded tape. Press the ends of the twill tape ¼" to the wrong side. Starting at one end of the tape, topstitch close to the edges, continuing across the mask and to the opposite end of the tape (**photo D**). Repeat for the remaining side edge.

4. ***If you would like to have ribbon ties on the sides of the mask,*** pin an interfacing piece to the wrong side of mask body and lining piece. Place mask body and lining right sides together and sew around all edges, leaving an opening along one long edge for turning. *Optional:* add a paper clip for nose shaping before adding the binding; see page 45. Turn the mask right side out and press. Press 3 pleats into the mask, folding and pressing all layers (**photo B**). Baste the pleats in place along the short ends. Centering the ribbon on the short edge, pin the ribbon to the mask. Topstitch the ribbon to the mask (**photo E**). Repeat for the remaining side edge.

C

D

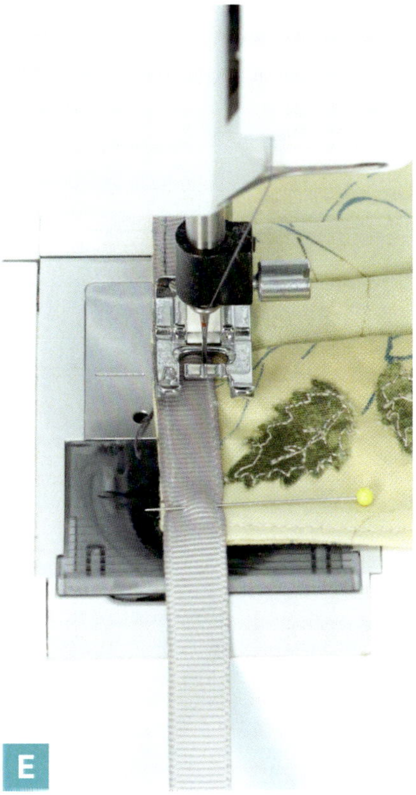

E

General Instructions

Making Binding For Ties

1. Press the short ends of one strip ¼" to the wrong side (**photo A**).
2. Fold tie in half lengthwise and press (**photo B**).
3. Open the strip and fold the raw edges to the center fold; press (**photo C**).
4. Fold the strip in half lengthwise again and press, completing the tie (**photo D**).
5. Repeat Steps 1–4 to make the remaining tie.

A

B

C

D

Adding A Paper Clip

Adding a paper clip allows the center front of the mask to be shaped around the nose.

1. Use pliers to straighten the paper clip. Bend the ends back on themselves so that the ends are not pointed or sharp (**photo E**).

2. You are going to make a stitched "casing" for the paper clip. Set your sewing machine for a wide, somewhat loose zigzag stitch. Sew zigzag stitches on the seam allowances at the top center of the mask. Make sure to catch both seam allowances and to extend the zigzag stitches about 2" toward each side of center. Slide the paper clip under the zigzag stitches (**photo F**).

TIPS

- Use contrasting fabric for the mask lining so you can tell which side is the inside.
- Use what you have for fabric—scraps, t-shirts, or pre-cuts such as fat quarters.

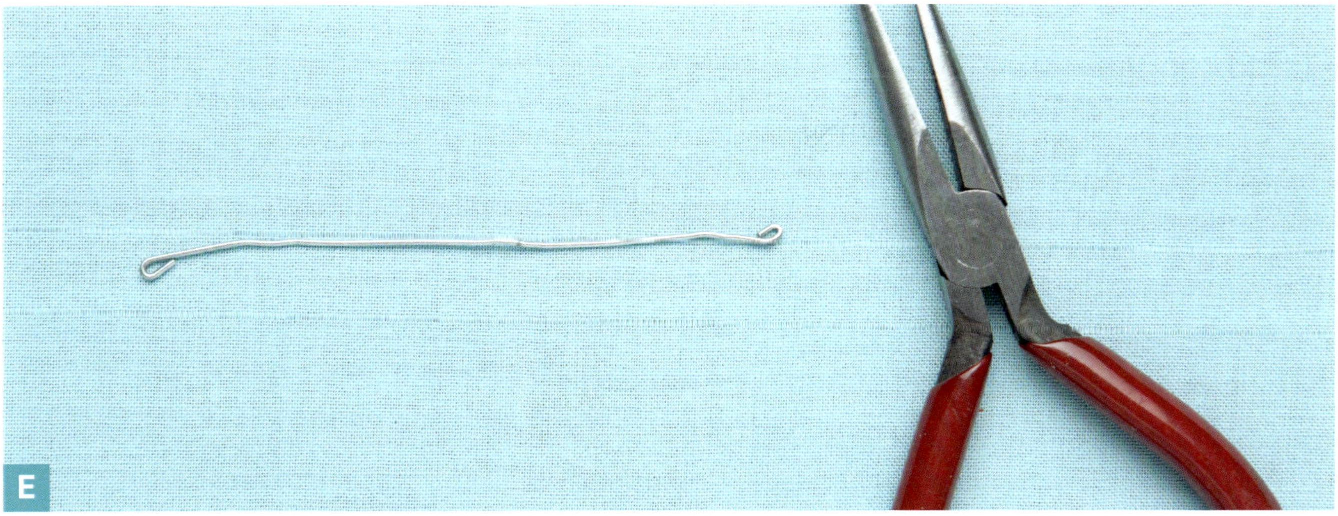

E

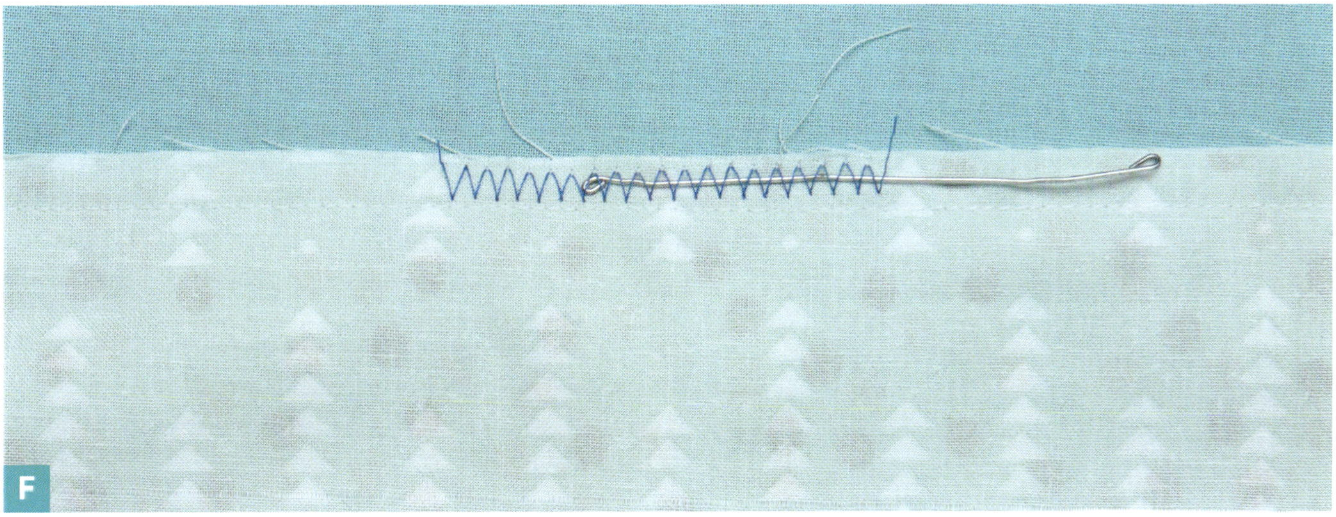

F

Patterns

Patterns are also available as SVG files to be used with an electronic cutting machine. Here are the links:

bit.ly/L7741_SmAdultMask
bit.ly/L7741_LgAdultMask
bit.ly/L7741_ChildMask

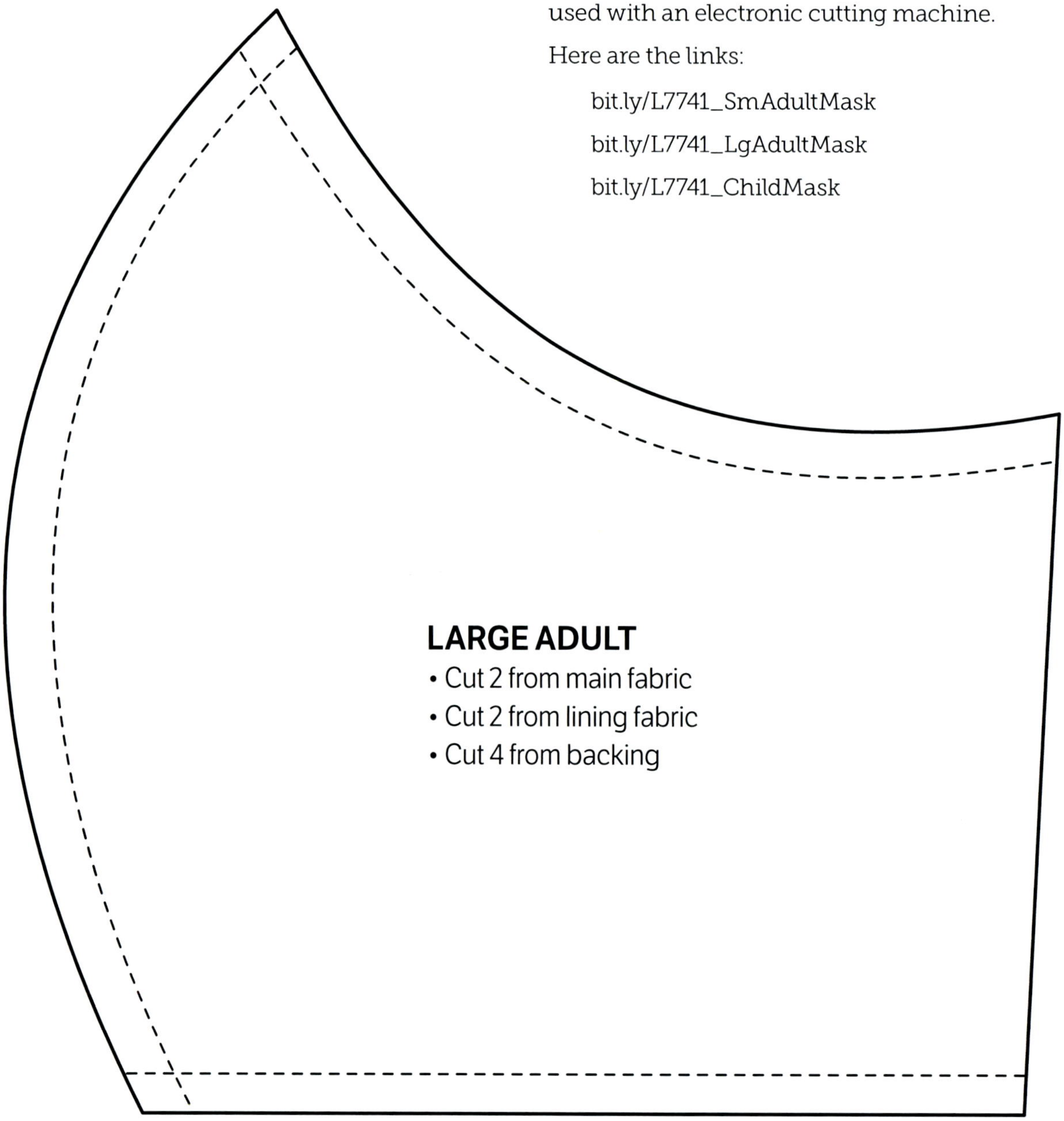

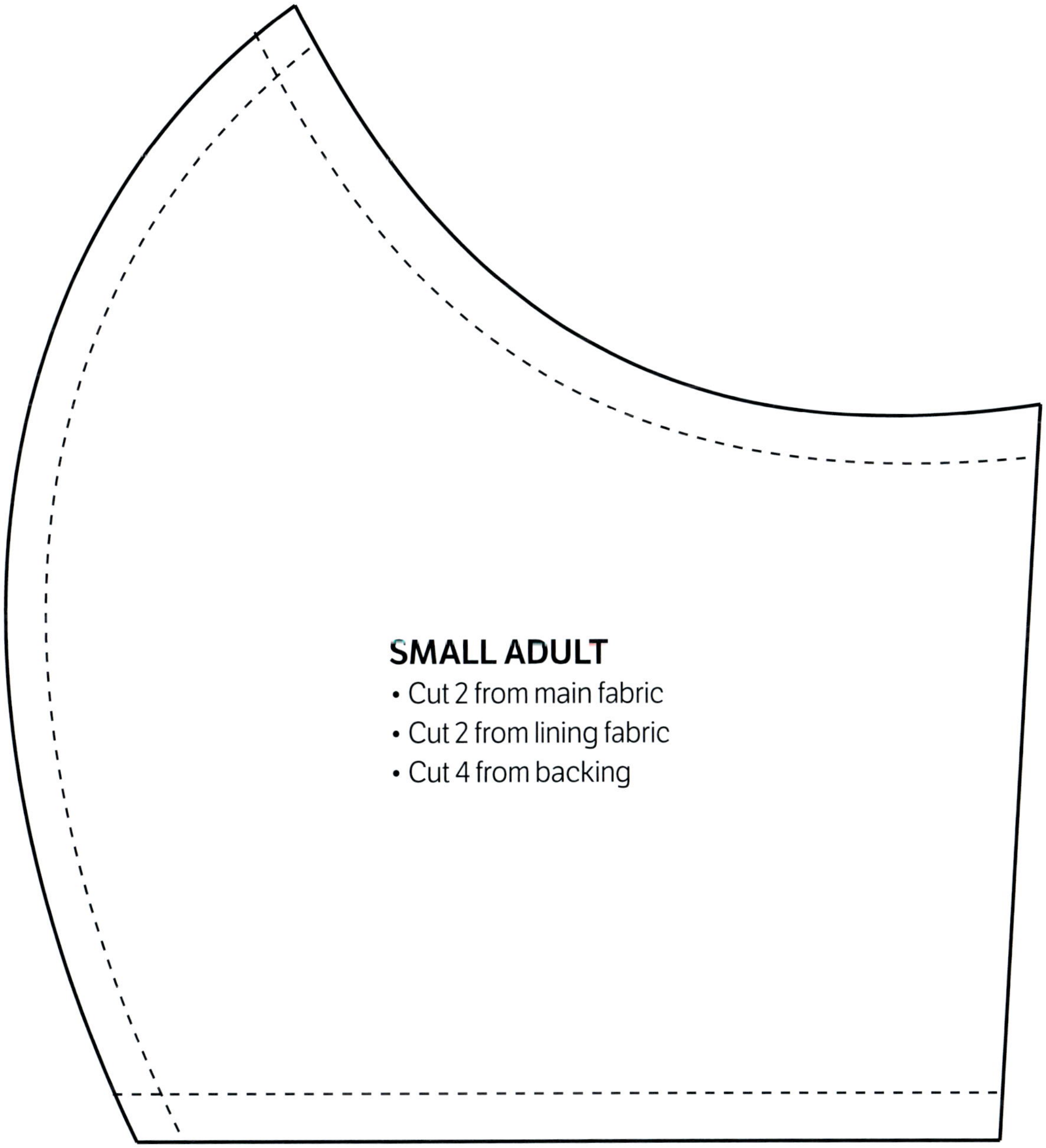
SMALL ADULT
• Cut 2 from main fabric
• Cut 2 from lining fabric
• Cut 4 from backing

Patterns

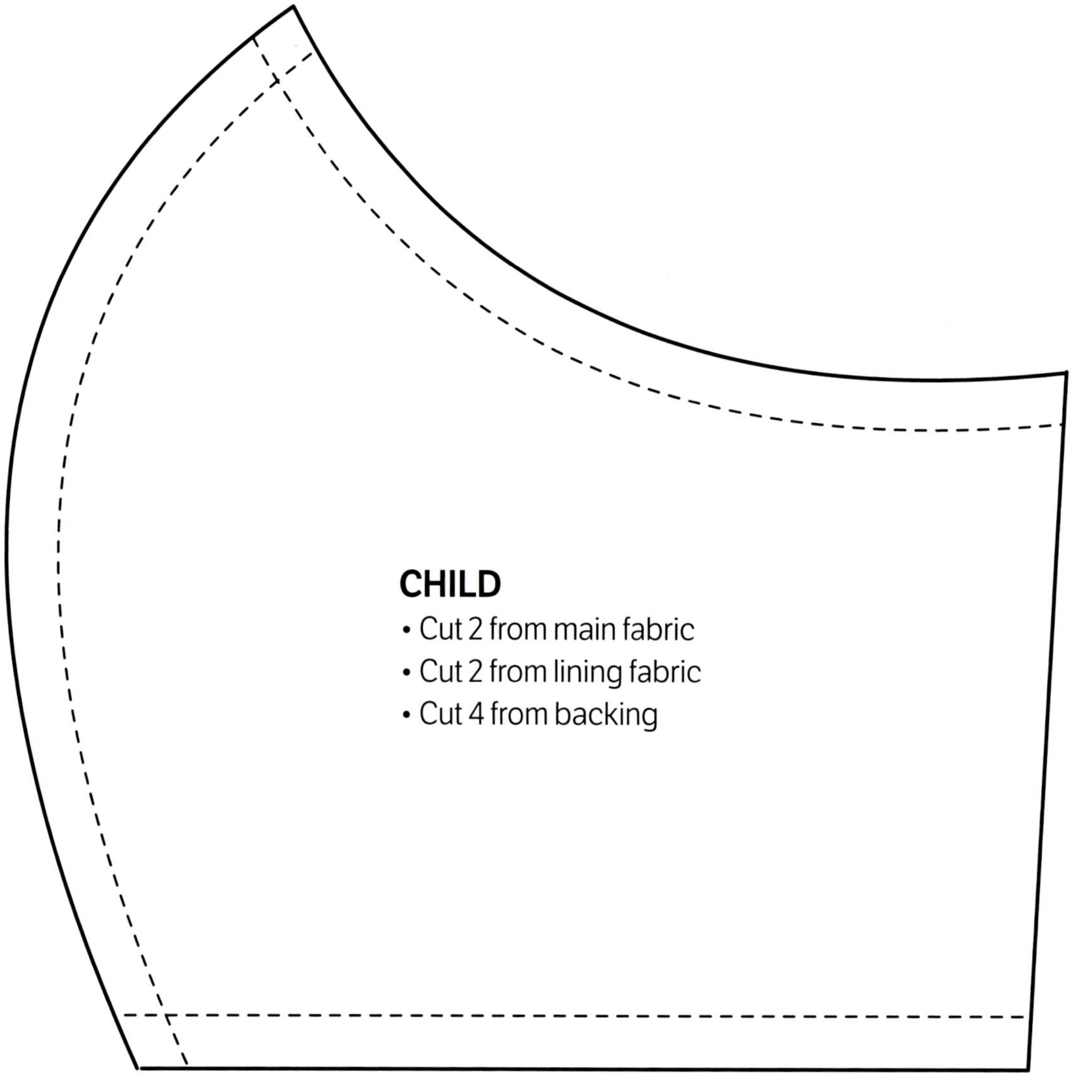

Production Team: Project Designers – Heidi Burroughs, Lee Fisher, Susan Fouts, and Denise Russell; Graphic Designer – Michael Douglas; Graphic Artists – Gary Hutcheson and Steph Johnson; Photography Stylist – Lori Wenger; Photographers – Rob Karman and Jason Masters

We have made every effort to ensure that these instructions are accurate and complete. We cannot, however, be responsible for human error, typographical mistakes, or variations in individual work.

Copyright © 2020 by Leisure Arts, Inc., 104 Champs Blvd., STE 100, Maumelle, AR 72113-6738, www.leisurearts.com. All rights reserved. This publication is protected under federal copyright laws. Reproduction or distribution of this publication or any other Leisure Arts publication, including publications which are out of print, is prohibited unless specifically authorized. This includes, but is not limited to, any form of reproduction or distribution on or through the Internet, including posting, scanning, or e-mail transmission.

Made in U.S.A.